Hispanic Heritage

Hispanic Heritage

Title List

Latino Folklore and Culture

Stories of Family, Traditions of Pride

by Ellyn Sanna

Mason Crest Publishers
Philadelphia

Mason Crest Publishers Inc.

370 Reed Road, Broomall, Pennsylvania 19008

(866) MCP-BOOK (toll free)

www.masoncrest.com

14 13 12 11 10 09 08 07   10 9 8 7 6 5 4 3

Library of Congress Cataloging-in-Publication Data

Sanna, Ellyn, 1958–
  Latino folklore and culture : stories of family, traditions of pride / by Ellyn Sanna.
      p. cm. — (Hispanic heritage)
  Includes index.
  ISBN 1-59084-932-9 ISBN 1-59084-924-8 (series)
  1. Latin Americans—Folklore. 2. Latin Americans—Social life and customs. 3. Tales—
Latin America. I. Title. II. Hispanic heritage (Philadelphia, Pa.)
  GR114.S35 2005
  398'.089'68073—dc22
                          2004024248

Cover design and interior design by Dianne Hodack.
Produced by Harding House Publishing Service, Inc., Vestal, NY.
www.hardinghousepages.com
Chapter 5 adapted from Kenneth McIntosh's contribution.
Printed in the Hashemite Kingdom of Jordan.

Contents

Introduction

by José E. Limón, Ph.D.

ven before there was a United States, Hispanics were present in what would become this country. Beginning in the sixteenth century, Spanish explorers traversed North America, and their explorations encouraged settlement as early as the sixteenth century in what is now northern New Mexico and Florida, and as late as the mid-eighteenth century in what is now southern Texas and California.

Later, in the nineteenth century, following Spain's gradual withdrawal from the New World, Mexico in particular established its own distinctive presence in what is now the southwestern part of the United States, a presence reinforced in the first half of the twentieth century by substantial immigration from that country. At the close of the nineteenth century, the U.S. war with Spain brought Cuba and Puerto Rico into an interactive relationship with the United States, the latter in a special political and economic affiliation with the United States even as American power influenced the course of almost every other Latin American country.

The books in this series remind us of these historical origins, even as each explores the present reality of different Hispanic groups. Some of these books explore the contemporary social origins—what social scientists call the "push" factors—behind the accelerating Hispanic immigration to America: political instability, economic underdevelopment and crisis, environmental degradation, impoverished or wholly absent educational systems, and other circumstances contribute to many Latin Americans deciding they will be better off in the United States.

And, for the most part, they will be. The vast majority come to work and work very hard, in order to earn better wages than they would back home. They fill significant labor needs in the U.S. economy and contribute to the economy through lower consumer prices and sales taxes.

When they leave their home countries, many immigrants may initially fear that they are leaving behind vital and important aspects of their home cultures: the Spanish language, kinship ties, food, music, folklore, and the arts. But as these books also make clear, culture is a fluid thing, and these native cultures are not only brought to America, they are also replenished in the United States in fascinating and novel ways. These books further suggest to us that Hispanic groups enhance American culture as a whole.

Our country—especially the young, future leaders who will read these books—can only benefit by the fair and full knowledge these authors provide about the socio-historical origins and contemporary cultural manifestations of America's Hispanic heritage.

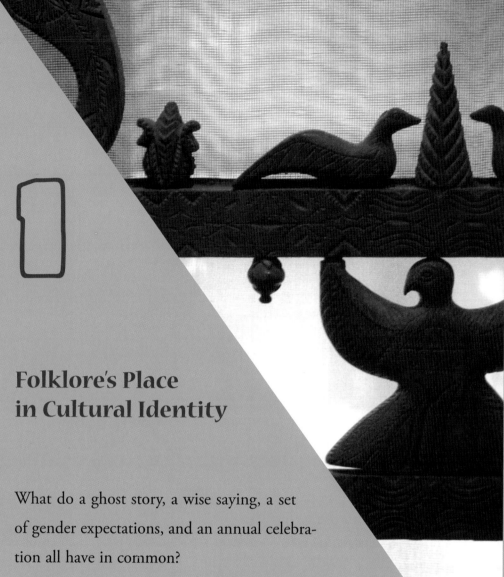

Folklore's Place in Cultural Identity

What do a ghost story, a wise saying, a set of gender expectations, and an annual celebration all have in common?

They are all part of the package that makes up Latino identity. A common folklore helps create the shape of Hispanic culture. It helps define an important group of Americans.

Artwork

Paintings from El Santuario de Chimayo reveal much about Latino culture and folklore.

Nineteenth-century Latino folk art often portrayed Mary. Here her triangular skirt served as a reminder of the mountains, which figured in Native folk beliefs.

What Is Culture?

hen *sociologists* talk about culture, they are referring to the patterns of knowledge, beliefs, and behaviors a group of people passes along from generation to generation. These patterns include sets of shared attitudes, values, goals, and practices. They have to do with the group's routines, the actions and thoughts that define people's everyday existence. Someone who belongs to a particular culture may be unaware of the practices that are unique to her culture. She takes these patterns of behavior for granted—they are simply the way things are done—but for an outsider looking in, these cultural traits will be very obvious.

Each group of people creates some form of culture. For example, a family will have its own unique culture, as will a workplace. Usually, however, we think of culture in terms of larger groups, such as nations or ethnic groups. Hispanic Americans are part of the larger American culture, but they also share a unique cultural heritage that is rich with folklore.

What Is Folklore?

he word "folklore" means the traditions that are learned and passed along by ordinary people as part of the fabric of their lives and culture. Folklore may be handed down in verbal form, like the *urban legend* that is told between friends, each one adding the assurance that the story "really" happened to a friend of a friend. Or it may be the songs and sayings grandchildren learn from their grandparents. It is the knowledge people acquire from those around them about the world and the meaning of life.

This knowledge isn't the kind learned in school; instead, it is picked up at family celebrations and community parties from friends and family. Folklore is culture shared by others in the community—and individual lives are built upon this shared understanding of how group members should act and what they should believe.

sociologists: scientists who study the origin, development, and structure of human societies and the behavior of individuals within them.

urban legend: a story that might have begun with some truth that has been embellished and retold until it has become a myth with little or no resemblance to the original story or the truth.

ethnicity: someone's
ethnic affiliation. The
characteristics of a na-
tional, linguistic, or
cultural group.

linguistic: relating to
language or languages.

The family is the smallest community unit that passes along folklore; folklore is communicated at meals and at bedtime, on holidays and ordinary days, through prayers and songs and stories. Folklore helps children develop a sense of belonging, first to their families and then, as they grow older, to the larger community. Rather than being adrift in the shifting sea of twenty-first-century life, individuals with strong cultural backgrounds are anchored by tradition.

For Latinos, these anchors tie them to their families, to the larger Hispanic community, and to a long and rich historical heritage. In the sometimes dangerous and ever-changing modern world, folklore tells Latinos who they are. It provides them with a sense of identity.

What Is Identity?

Identity is the way a person perceives herself, and it is made up of many factors. For example, gender—whether you are female or male—is a fundamental form of identity. Things like *ethnicity*, religion, and nationality also play a large role. Folklore and cultural background help many Hispanic Americans form their sense of who they are.

A street vendor sells Hispanic folk crafts.

What Does It Mean
to Be Latino or Hispanic?
(And Is There a Difference?)

eople from the Spanish-speaking countries of the Western Hemisphere may struggle to accommodate the term "Hispanic" with their individual identities. It is a term given to a certain *linguistic* group, a label for a type of group identity. In North America, people usually use the word Hispanic to describe any person who is descended from Spanish-speaking ancestors but who does not come from Spain.

This definition, however, includes many different groups of people from numerous countries. The United States has a large Spanish-speaking population, and many countries in the Americas have Spanish as their official language. These regions, of course, did not always speak Spanish.

In the 1400s, the people of Spain were the first in a great wave of Europeans to come to the Americas. The Spanish *conquistadors* eventually claimed huge portions of land in the Caribbean and South, Central, and North America. The conquest of the Americas was a brutal attack on the Native people who already lived here. Millions of people throughout the Americas were killed by the wars, poverty, and diseases the Europeans brought.

The first Spanish conquistadors and settlers were men. They generally came looking for riches, like gold. Some of these men

These countries in the Western Hemisphere are Spanish-speaking: Mexico; the Central American countries of Guatemala, El Salvador, Honduras, Nicaragua, Costa Rica, and Panama; the Caribbean countries of Cuba and the Dominican Republic; and the South American countries of Venezuela, Colombia, Ecuador, Peru, Bolivia, Paraguay, Uruguay, Argentina, and Chile. Spanish is also the first language of Puerto Rico, which is a protectorate of the United States.

Ruins left behind by the sophisticated Native cultures of the Western Hemisphere

A re-creation of a Spanish settler's home

married Native women and had families. These Spanish settlers were now in a land very different from their home, and they adopted Native practices and ways of life more suited to this land. Meanwhile, immigration from Spain increased, with whole families now settling in the Americas. Many people came as missionaries to *convert* the Native people to Christianity. The Spanish people (and later other Europeans) also brought slaves from Africa. These various African cultures further influenced the Spanish settlers and their descendants. Over hundreds of years, new cultures developed that combined aspects of Spanish, Native, and African heritages, while responding to new conditions in the Americas.

Today, although Spanish is the official language of many American countries and regions, their citizens cannot be called "Spanish." Spanish-speaking people in the Americas have a very different heritage and culture than people have in Spain. In fact, many Spanish-speaking people in the Americas today would have to trace their ancestry back hundreds of years to find a link with Spain. Others have no Spanish link at all (except for the language they speak). To call everyone who speaks the Spanish language "Spanish" would make no more sense than calling all English-speaking Americans "English."

In the 1980s, the U.S. government developed the term "Hispanic" to describe anyone in the Americas who spoke Spanish as his first language or had Spanish heritage. The term is generally only used in the United States and Canada, and not everyone is happy with it. Some people don't appreciate the U.S. government labeling them. They would rather define themselves than have a government body spell out their identity for them.

After all, the Americas are a huge and diverse place. Because "Hispanic" is a linguistic grouping, it includes people of many different nationalities, ethnicities, races, and cultural backgrounds. Many people don't like the way the term lumps everyone together. Furthermore, people from the Americas have mixed ancestry. The word "Hispanic" emphasizes a person's Spanish heritage without acknowledging other aspects of his background.

Some people are comfortable using the word to help define their identity; some are not. The term "Hispanic" is favored by the majority of people from Cuban and Puerto

gringos: in Spain and Latin America, a derogatory term for an English-speaking foreigner.

Rican descent residing in Florida, and is acceptable to most Hispanics on the East Coast of the United States. In the Midwest, however, and in California, the term "Latino" is favored.

D. H. Figueredo, who teaches college courses in Latino literature, describes the origins of the word "Latino": "Latino is a Spanish word. It has a gender: Latino for male, Latina for female. It is short for Latinoamericano, thus it looks more towards Latin America than to Spain. In the United States, the term was not coined by the *gringos*, but emerged from the *gente*, the people themselves."

The very fact that Hispanics—or Latinos—cannot agree on which term to use for themselves demonstrates their diversity. They come from a multitude of widespread nations, and as a result, many U.S. descendants of immigrants prefer to think of their identity in terms of national origin. Just as some people still think of themselves as "Irish" or "Italian," even though they are the second or third generation born in America, Hispanics often define themselves by such national terms as *Salvadoraña* (a female Salvadoran) or *Guatemalteco* (a male Guatemalan).

Common Threads

nd yet despite their differences, Hispanic Americans are woven together with recurring threads. They share many of the same stories, the same faith, and the same values.

Wise Words

Latino *dichos* (dee-choes) are proverbs (or wise sayings) that have been quoted for centuries. No one remembers who was the first person to say them; they've been a part of Hispanic folklore for as long as anyone can remember. Some may have come from Spain, some from Native wise people, some from Africa, and some from the Muslim world that once ruled Spain. Whatever the original source, these proverbs have come to express the philosophy and values of the Hispanic people. They manifest the Latino culture's character and spirit.

Cada persona es un mundo.
Each individual is a separate world.

Cortesía de boca, mucho vale y poco cuesta.
A courteous mouth is worth a great deal and costs little.

El que va despacio llega lejos.
He who goes slowly goes far.

El que hace más de lo que puede, hace más do lo que debe.
The person who does more than she is able, does more than she ought.

El trabajo revive al hombre.
Work revives the man.

La caridad por uno empieza.
Charity begins with oneself.

Colorful Latino fabrics

From group to group, the concept of family and the roles each person plays within that context look very similar. The bright patterns of folklore and family create the colorful fabric of Hispanic life. As you gain an understanding of how these patterns are constructed, you may catch a glimpse of what it means to be Latino.

Habla Español

gente (hane-tay): people

cuentos (kwane-toes): stories

Latinos Today

t the beginning of the twenty-first century, Latinos have become the dominant minority group in the United States. In January 2003, the Census Bureau announced, "Hispanics have surpassed blacks as the nation's largest minority group." The same report provided the following details on the U.S. population: "Hispanics now comprise nearly 13 percent of the U.S. population, which grew to 284.8 million in July 2001. Blacks make up 12.7 percent of the nation's population. Asians are the next largest minority group after blacks and Hispanics, at about 12.1 million, or 4 percent of the population. Whites remained the largest single population group, numbering about 199.3 million, nearly 70 percent of all U.S. residents." More recently, the Census Bureau reported that the Latino population in the United States nearly doubled between 1990 and 2004—from 22.4 million to almost 40 million.

Americans with ancient ancestral roots in both Spain and the Americas have taken what's best and most vibrant in those traditions and married them to the energy and freedom of the United States. They have faced discrimination and hardship, but they have fought for their rights on the job, in school, and on the street. Although many battles remain to be fought, Latinos today are seizing success in virtually every area of American life.

2

The Crying Woman: Symbol of the Latino People

Miguel knew he'd had too much to drink when the dark street seemed to dip and sway beneath his feet. His apartment was only a few blocks ahead, and he tried to keep his steps straight, but he kept stumbling on the cracked pavement. Between the buildings' black shapes, he caught the dark glimmer of the river, running slow and silent in the fitful moonlight. He shivered and longed for the noise of a car, a sound of a radio, anything to indicate he wasn't the only human being alive in the empty night. His drunken mind grasped onto the thought that there was something unnatural about the quiet, as though some huge and hulking beast were holding its breath, waiting to pounce. At least he was nearly home.

Carmen would be angry because he'd stayed out late again. She might even smell the scent of Juana's perfume on his skin—but eventually, he knew she'd forgive him and let him sleep.

As he turned the corner toward his apartment, he caught a glimpse of movement. Someone else was out in the night, walking along the river, and Miguel let out a sigh of relief. But as he came closer, he stopped short, frozen, the gasp of his breath harsh in the silence. The shape ahead of him was not the late-night pedestrian he had expected. Instead, something pale and hazy was drifting beside the river, trailing cold white tatters behind it.

He squeezed his eyes shut and then opened them again, hoping if he could force his blurry gaze to focus he would see that the white shape was only a wisp of river mist. But it wasn't. Without a noise, the thing floated closer, and now he could clearly make out the face of a woman tipped up toward him. She was beautiful, but her features were twisted with a horrified sorrow, and her skin was pale as ice.

"Noooo." The wailing voice was so soft that at first Miguel thought it was a sudden breeze, stirring the weeds that grew along the riverbank. Then the sound gained volume, growing until it filled the night. Miguel clapped his hands over his ears, trying to shut out the woman's terrible grief. She raised her hand and pointed directly at him.

Miguel stared back into eyes that were as dark and empty as holes. He thought of his wife's trusting face, and then he remembered the kisses he had exchanged tonight with Juana, the girl he had met at the bar. A flood of guilt and remorse washed over him. "I'm sorry," he whispered.

The pale face turned away from him, as though he were no longer important to her. Instead, she leaned over the river, her cries floating through the silent night as she seemed to search the dark water for something she had lost, something infinitely precious, something she could never hope to regain no matter how long she searched. The sorrow in her voice made tears spring to his eyes.

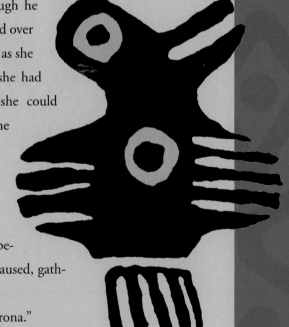

And then she was gone. Miguel stumbled quickly into his apartment building and let out a long breath as he heard the heavy door thud behind him. On the stairs up to his apartment, he paused, gathering his shattered wits.

"La Llorona," he whispered. "I just saw La Llorona."

He'd heard the old stories whispered ever since he was a child, but he had never believed them. Now he knew they were true.

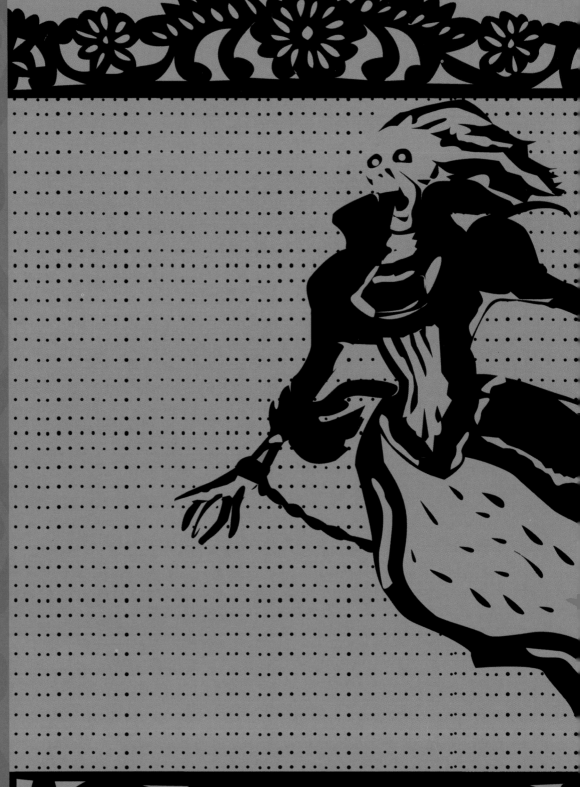

The Legend of La Llorona

he people of Hispanic America have told and retold the story of La Llorona for hundreds of years. The sad tale cannot be erased from their memories, no matter how many years pass. Many people swear it is far more than a folktale. They believe an ancient truth lies at the heart of the story.

The Urban Legend Version

inda was a single mother who lived in the poor part of town. She had grown up in poverty, and now she was raising her children in the same environment. Her children had no father, and Linda's own father had refused to have anything to do with her.

Then one day Linda met Luis, a handsome and well-to-do man. Luis and Linda became lovers, and Linda hoped he would marry her. However, as the months went by, Luis made no mention of marriage, and finally Linda began dropping hints. After several weeks, Luis exploded with anger. "I'll never marry you," he shouted. "I don't want to be weighed down with another man's children!"

Shortly after that, Luis stopped seeing Linda. When she went looking for him, she heard two men joking about Luis and his new girlfriend, a woman from a nearby town who didn't have the responsibility of two children hanging around her neck. Stricken with jealousy and sorrow, Linda became convinced that her children were standing between her and her happiness. She took them to the lake and held them beneath the water until their cries turned to silence.

Almost immediately, Linda came to her senses and tried to revive her children—but it was too late. Neighbors took her dead children from her arms and buried them. Linda, however, refused to leave the lake. She haunted the water's edge, sobbing and moaning, until one day the townspeople found her lifeless body stretched out cold and limp on the shore. They buried her beside her children.

But on dark nights, they still hear her voice, crying for her lost children. And men who have been cheating on their wives or girlfriends are sometimes seen following a beautiful woman with long hair. Oftentimes, those men are never seen again.

Some say La Llorona has her roots in Spain, where her story was told before the conquistadors ever came to the Americas. Others, however, say the Spanish found the story waiting for them in the "New World" and mixed it with their own legends.

The Eastern Hemisphere, the "Old World"

The Western Hemisphere, the "New World"

New World or Old World?

hen Europeans crossed the Atlantic Ocean, they referred to North and South America as the "New World." Today, many people still speak of the Americas as the New World, while they call Europe the "Old World." From the perspective of the people already living in the Americas when the Europeans arrived, however, the terms might just as well have been reversed. The Native groups—often called Indians—would have thought of the Europeans as coming from a strange, new world, while the land the Indians called home would have been the old, familiar world.

The goddess Cihuacoatl

The Goddess Cihuacoatl

According to the early chronicles of Aztec mythology, the goddess Cihuacoatl sometimes appeared on dark nights, dressed in white robes that trailed behind her like a cloud, while she carried a dead baby in her arms. In the months before the arrival of the Europeans, the Aztecs were said to have heard Cihuacoatl moaning and sobbing in the darkness. "Oh my children," she cried, "your destruction is coming. Flee far away! Oh my little ones, where can I find safety for you?"

Modern street graffiti portrays La Llorona's ghostly image.

Cihuacoatl was the ancient Aztec goddess of the earth, of war, and of birth. She was the patron of midwives and carried a papoose on her back—but inside the cradle was a sacrificial knife, swaddled in cloth. Her face was covered with white chalk, and she wore a white dress. The lower part of her face was a bare jawbone, representing her connection to death. She was thought to be a harbinger of tragedy and catastrophe—and yet her presence also signified birth and the hope of new life.

In the years that followed, as the Natives of the Americas were forced to surrender to their Spanish conquerors, the story grew. The life of a woman called Doña Marina—or La Malinche—gave historical flesh to the ancient legend.

La Malinche

La Malinche (pronounced "mah-leen-chay") was a Native from the Gulf Coast of Mexico, one of twenty slave women given as gifts to the triumphant Spaniards. She was an intelligent woman, fluent in both the *Nahuatl* language (spoken by most of the Natives of Central Mexico) and the Maya language (which one of the Spanish priests un-

primary sources: accounts by eyewitnesses or the first persons to record an event.

La Malinche's real name may have been "Malinalli," an Aztec word that means "grass." The suffix "-tzin" was added to names as a way of showing respect, making her name "Malintzin"—which the Spaniards pronounced as "Malinche." When the twenty slave women were handed over to the Spanish, Cortés insisted that they be baptized as Christians. At her baptism, La Malinche was given the Spanish name "Marina." The word "Doña" was added as a term of respect, indicating the high regard the Spaniards had for Cortés's mistress.

derstood). Soon, Hernán Cortés was using her as his interpreter, and within a few months, La Malinche had learned enough of her master's language to translate directly from Nahuatl into Spanish.

La Malinche went on to play a central role in the conquest of Mexico. Apparently, she was not only Cortés's interpreter but his advisor and lover as well. After God, Cortés said, Doña Marina was the main reason for his success. *Primary sources*

A billboard advertises a modern movie based on the legend of La Llorona.

make clear that La Malinche's influence and intelligence were immense. Native drawings that record the events of the time rarely portray Cortés without La Malinche poised beside his ear; sometimes, she is even shown alone, apparently directing events under her own authority.

LLORONA

The Historical Record

La Malinche's story made its way to the twenty-first century by word of mouth, passed down through the generations, a story that was told and retold. Historical records, however, confirm at least pieces of her story. The conquistador Andrés de Tapia refers to Doña Marina in his written accounts, as does Cortés's biographer, Gómara. Díaz del Castillo gives the most detailed record of Doña Marina in his romantic chronicles of the time.

According to Díaz, La Malinche was a princess from the borderlands between the Aztec empire and the Yucatan, where the Maya lived. When the princess was still a young girl, her father died, and her mother remarried. Her new stepfather wanted to rid himself of his stepdaughter, and so he sold her to a Mayan slave trader. Eventually, when she was about fourteen, she was given to the Spaniards. She died around 1529.

Many of the Native people felt La Malinche was a traitor to her own people. Aztec *nationalists* refer to a "*malinchista*" as a person who betrays race and country by mixing with European blood and culture. Some modern historians, however, believe that in fact, La Malinche *saved* her people. The Europeans who settled further north eventually displaced the Native cultures so completely that only faint traces of Native influences can be seen across English-speaking North America—while meanwhile, to the south, the Spanish mixed with the Native people, forming a new and unique culture. Without the influence of La Malinche, an intelligent *intermediary* who was able to shape events on both sides, the Spanish conquest might have been far more violent and destructive. Although the Spanish conquistadors destroyed the Native governments, much of Native history and culture still remains, thanks, perhaps, to the *diplomatic* genius of La Malinche.

Cortés clearly respected his Native mistress's intelligence and abilities. She gave birth to his son, Don Martín Cortés, but in the end, Hernán Cortés married off his lover to one of his lieutenants. According to some historical records, Doña Marina had a daughter with her Spanish husband and traveled with her new family to Central America, where she died of an illness when she was only twenty-three years old. Legend, however, tells another story.

These folk traditions say that La Malinche's Spanish lover abandoned her. Some say he left her to marry a noble-born Spanish girl; other accounts tell that Cortés did not want the responsibility of his illegitimate child. In either case, the Native woman became crazy with desperation and sorrow . . . and drowned her children in the river. She then took her own life.

But her spirit continues to haunt the cities and *pueblos* of

nationalists: those who have an excessive devotion to their country and its interests.

intermediary: a go-between; someone who tries to bring about an agreement.

diplomatic: showing tact and skill in dealing with people.

embodies: represents an abstract concept in physical form.

North America. She is condemned to wander for eternity, weeping and wailing as she searches for her lost children. Her legend has endured for more than three centuries.

A Symbol of Latino Identity

Although La Llorona is a tragic and horrifying legend, many Latinos also claim her as a positive symbol of their identity. Because La Malinche gave birth to the first *mestizo*, she is considered to be the mother of a new race—Latin Americans, a group of people like no other in the world. Latinos see themselves as orphans of La Llorona, the offspring of the marriage between the Native Indians and the Spanish conquerors. The ancient legend gives shape to Latinos' anger and bitterness—but it also *embodies* their pride in their own unique identity.

Habla Español

La Llorona (lah yo-ro-nah): "the crying woman"

mestizo (may-stee-so): "mixed-race," part European and part Native Indian

pueblos (pwayb-low): towns, villages

La Raza

Many Latinos speak of "*la Raza*," a term that refers to all descendants of the Spanish–Native encounter in the Americas. The term is a way of claiming their distinct cultural heritage, while looking toward the future with pride and hope. "*La Raza* is the affirmation of the most basic ingredient of our personality," writes José Angel Gutiérrez, "the brownhood of our Indian ancestors wedded to all the other skin colors of mankind. . . . As children of *La Raza*, we are heirs of a spiritual and biological miracle."

"*Viva la Raza!*" (Long live the People!) is frequently chanted at the openings and closings of Latino concerts, celebrations, and political meetings. And October 12 (officially referred to as Columbus Day by the American government) is celebrated throughout Latin America as *Día de la Raza* (Day of the People), the day when, according to tradition, the first European encountered the Native Indian world of the Americas, thus giving birth to the Hispanic culture.

Macho Men

La Malinche's lover, Hernán Cortés, was a hard man. He mistreated even the woman he loved; he had many lovers and was faithful to none; and he was too strong to take any notice of the weak who got in his way. Cortés grabbed whatever he wanted from life. In many ways, he fit the *stereotype* of what it means to be a Hispanic man. La Llorona may have punished the men who followed in his footsteps—but the strong and faithless man remained a constant in Latino tradition.

stereotype: an oversimplified idea held by one person or a group about another person or group, often based on incorrect and incomplete information.

45

Latinos have a word for their masculine traditions: *machismo*. According to the *Dictionary of Mexican Cultural Code Words:*

Machismo meant the *repudiation* of all "feminine" virtues such as unselfishness, kindness, frankness and truthfulness. It meant being willing to lie without *compunction*, to be suspicious, envious, jealous, malicious, *vindictive*, brutal and finally, to be willing to fight and kill without hesitation to protect one's manly image. *Machismo* meant that a man could not let anything detract from his image of himself as a man's man, regardless of the suffering it brought on himself and the women around him. . . . The proof of every man's manliness was his ability to completely dominate his wife and children, to have sexual relations with any woman he wanted, to never let anyone question, *deprecate* or attempt to thwart his manhood, and never to reveal his true feelings to anyone lest they somehow take advantage of him.

Many sociologists believe these characteristics are often typical of a patriarchal culture—one where men are the authority figures and women have little financial, political, or social power. This type of culture was brought to Latin America by its Spanish conquerors.

Machismo may have a harsh and unappealing face—but for many Latino men and women, it also has a powerful and charming aspect that is hard to resist. The irresistible Latin lover, the *insatiable* and *invincible* man, are themes that show up again and again in Latino traditions and folklore.

A Latino Folktale

here was once a rich man who had five sons—Pedro, Diego, José, Juan, and Manuel. The brothers had everything they needed, and yet they always wanted to have just a little bit more. So one day, the brothers decided to set out on a trip to seek still greater fortune for themselves. Even their littlest brother, Manuel, would come with them, for he was as brave and manly as the others.

repudiation: rejection.

compunction: feelings of shame and regret about having done something wrong.

vindictive: feeling, showing, or doing something to hurt someone or as vengeance.

deprecate: to express condemnation for something or someone.

insatiable: incapable of being filled.

invincible: incapable of being harmed or destroyed.

The five brothers set out on their journey. They had not gone far, when they came to a place where the road forked into five separate paths. "Which way shall we go?" Manuel asked.

Pedro, being the oldest, assigned a different road to each of the brothers. "Let us each seek our fortune—and after one year, we will meet here again before we return to our father's house." So each brother set out on his own path.

Pedro came to the house of a professional thief. The man hired Pedro to be his companion, and he soon taught Pedro his trade. "No thief is my equal," the man boasted, "and I have never been caught." But within six months, Pedro knew three times what the master did. In fact, Pedro was so smooth he could take money right from under your nose.

Meanwhile, a great hunter had taken in the second brother, Diego. After only five days, Diego was a far better hunter than his master. After six months, Diego didn't even have to look when he aimed his gun. Animals fell dead whenever he fired.

Things were also going well for José. A doctor had taken him in and taught him everything about setting bones. After six months, if a man came to José with broken bones, José would set them so well that the man would seem to have never been hurt.

And little Manuel ended up at the house of a fortune-teller, where he learned to "see" what his father and each of his brothers were doing at all times. He too became far better than his master—and he knew exactly what each of his brothers had become in the time since he'd last seen them.

When he saw that his brothers had all gathered at the five corners where they had parted, Manuel packed up a suitcase full of gold he had earned and hurried to meet his brothers. They each had a suitcase of their own, all nearly bursting with coins. With their riches tucked under their arms, they went home to their father.

Not long after their homecoming, a rich man who lived nearby sent word to the five sons that his daughter had disappeared. He wanted the five rich and talented brothers to help him find her. "As soon as you bring her home, the one who works the hardest shall be her husband."

Many Latino males feel a strong sense of brotherhood.

The five brothers asked around and discovered that a giant named Old Long Arms had taken the girl. They set off immediately for the giant's *hacienda*. Little Manuel had a plan. "Pedro, you be the one who steals the princess. I'll tell you where she is hidden. And Diego can take a shot at the giant if need be."

The plan went smoothly, and the brothers escaped with the girl by boat. But Old Long Arms followed them and began smashing at their small craft with his giant fists. Quick as a flash, Diego shot the giant and killed him dead—but as he fell, he crashed into their boat, breaking the wood so that the water rushed in. José, however, soon realized that wood is not so different from bone, and he put the boat back together again before their clothes were more than damp.

When the brothers returned with the girl, her father jumped up and down with joy. "Which of these young men worked the hardest to free you?" the man asked.

When the girl had finished her story, her father scratched his head in puzzlement. All five of the brothers had worked hard.

"She's mine, she's mine!" they each shouted.

The girl's father laughed. "How silly you're being. A man may have five women, but no woman can have five men. Fortunately for you, I have five daughters—one for each of you."

And so the five brothers married and lived happily ever after, growing richer with each year.

he five brothers are "typical" Latino men—sometimes violent, occasionally *unscrupulous*, but always brave, powerful, and ultimately triumphant. They are winners every time. What woman could resist their strength and virility?

Of course, in today's world, authoritarian and aggressive men don't go over as well as they did before the days of *feminism*. Human rights demand that all people—men and women alike—be treated with equal respect, their individual strengths acknowledged. Many modern Latinos reject traditional concepts of machismo; they work toward a more equal relationship between men and women.

Other Latinos, however, look at things a bit differently. A grandchild who has grown up in a home with a strong but loving grandfather who "ruled" the family with wisdom and unabashed tenderness will see machismo far differently from the daughter whose father used cultural traditions to excuse his violent behavior toward his wife and children. In reality, there is no "typical" Latino male; each individual is unique, and cultural traditions are expressed differently in each person.

Modern Machismo

ome modern Latinos describe machismo in very different terms from the ones we've mentioned so far; they say it's the *epitome* of perfect manhood. The truly macho man is the one who supports and protects his family against all odds,

unscrupulous: unrestrained by moral principles.

feminism: the belief that women should have the same rights and opportunities as men.

epitome: a representative example of a type, class, or characteristic.

51

A Matter of Perspective

Several Hispanic authors question whether machismo's negative reputation might be partly a result of Anglo-Americans' misunderstanding of another culture. The style of conversation and body language that is expected of Latino men is quite different from what is expected of Anglo-Americans. And the same character traits can be interpreted differently, depending on your point of view.

MACHISMO

Anglo-American interpretation	Latino interpretation
loud	fervent
arrogant	confident
swaggering	energetic
violent	physically strong
aggressive	assertive
opinionated	determined
physical	passionate

Some see true machismo as being characterized by Latino men who protect their children and provide them with strong role models.

who disciplines his children to be honest and hardworking. From this perspective, machismo is a key factor in shaping a healthy family; it is a source of discipline that teaches children courtesy and high moral standards.

Jerry Tello, one of the founders of the National Compadres Network, a group of professional Latino men who work to instill positive values in young Latino men, points out that in Latin America, the word *macho* simply means "male," and a true man is someone who acts with respect, responsibility, and honor. The Compadres ("co-fathers") work to guide young Latino men to be *hombres nobles*—noble men.

ccording to the Compadres, a true man:

- is a man of his word
- has a sense of responsibility for his own well-being as well as for that of others in his circle
- rejects any form of abuse—physical, emotional, mental, or spiritual—to himself or others
- takes time to reflect, pray, and include ceremony in his life
- is sensitive to understanding
- is like a mirror, reflecting support and clarity to one another
- lives these values honestly, with love.

The Native Influence

Spain may have brought the tradition of strong, authoritarian manhood to Latin America—but it blended there with Native concepts. To be an hombre noble in the pre-Columbian Americas meant you were an honorable man of your word. It meant you respected both the spiritual and the human worlds, including women.

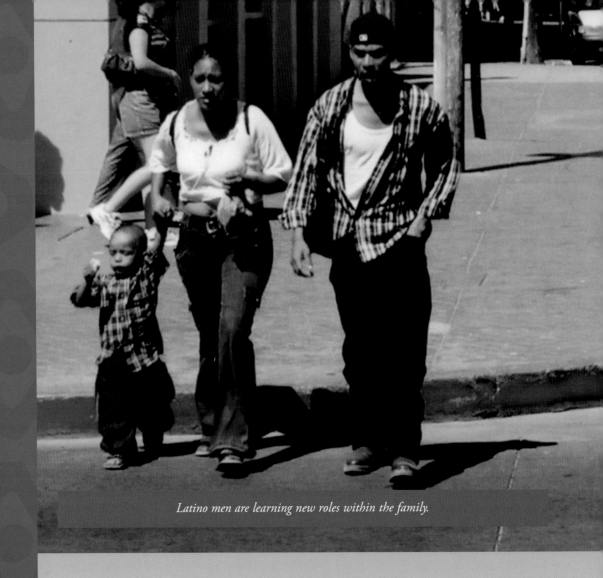

Latino men are learning new roles within the family.

tenacious: very determined or stubborn.

Modern Latinos have a double heritage: they are children of Spain and children of the Americas. Native American cultures had many traditions built around strong women who were given respect and appreciation—and Latino traditions have absorbed this concept that is seemingly so contradictory to machismo. Hispanic men may be loud, powerful, and courageous—but Latina women have their own brand of *tenacious* strength.

In a 1997 article in the *San Francisco Chronicle,* Roberto Rodriquez and Patrisia Gonzales write:

> As defined by U.S. society, the concept of "machismo" takes on strictly negative overtones. Being macho is considered synonymous with being a wife-beater, a philanderer, a drunk, a "bien gallo"—a fighter, like a rooster. This confuses young males. . . . And some young Latinos fulfill this distorted definition of manhood by acting out a false manliness in response to living in a foreign culture where they feel emasculated by racism and a lack of educational and job opportunities.

Habla Español

hacienda (ah-see-ane-dah): a large estate

hombre (ome-bray): man

noble (no-blay): noble

Strong Women

Once upon a time, there was young widow named Josefa who disguised herself as a man so she could go and see the world. As she journeyed through a great forest, she came upon a hunters' camp. "Come work with us," the men said. Of course, they had no idea she was a woman.

Every day, one hunter stayed behind in the camp to prepare the evening meal. When Josefa's turn came, the other hunters warned her, "Be careful. Someone keeps spilling the food when the camp is nearly empty."

Women's strength is portrayed in this Native sculpture.

"I'll watch," Josefa promised, and she kept her ears open while she cleaned the meat and cooked a stew. Sure enough, before too long, she heard the racket of jars being turned over and beans spattering across the ground. Josefa picked up a thick stick and ran toward the noise. She found an old woman flailing around among the bowls of food kept in the hunters' storehouse. When Josefa waved her stick and shouted, the old woman screeched and scuttled down a dark smelly hole at the edge of the hunters' camp.

When the other hunters returned, Josefa told them what had happened.

"We'll have to pull her out of that hole," they said. So they made a rope from strips of hide tied together, and they dropped it down into the cold wet darkness.

"It's an awfully deep hole," said the hunter who lowered himself, hand over hand, into the hole. His voice sounded small and hollow. "I've reached the bottom," he called, "and I'm going to—" But he never finished his sentence. Instead, he shinnied back up the rope as fast as he could. "I don't like it down there," he whispered when he reached the top.

The others laughed at him, and another hunter lowered himself into the hole. But before long, he too came scrabbling out again, his face as pale as chalk. A third hunter tried, and then the fourth, but each was too terrified to stay in the hole long enough to find the old woman.

"Why are you so scared?" Josefa asked. "What do you see?"

"A little white light," one of the hunters stammered.

Josefa shook her head at their cowardice. Then she picked up her stick and shinnied down the rope. When she reached the bottom of the dank hole, she saw the faraway twinkle of a white light, and she walked toward it slowly, tapping the ground ahead of her with her stick so she would not stumble.

As she grew closer to the light, she saw that it was actually five young women, each shining like a star. As Josefa put out her hand to them, they shrank back. "Don't touch us! Can't you see we've been enchanted? Judas captured us, and now he holds us captive. Our father is a king, but he can do nothing to save us. Judas's old wife brings us food, but we will never be free again."

"Nonsense!" Josefa said. "Come with me."

She led the five young women back to the rope and then helped them climb out of the hole. Before she could clamber up after them, she heard a noise behind her. When she looked over her shoulder, she saw the old woman coming toward her with her hands upraised like claws. "Pull up the rope!" she shouted, and the hunters whipped it out of sight. Josefa turned to face the old woman.

"Stop, thief!" the old woman screeched. "How dare you steal our princesses!"

Josefa swung her stick as hard as she could, and the old woman dropped to the ground in a pool of blood. Before Josefa could move, a bellow like a bull's echoed through the dark hole, and Judas appeared. "I smell blood!" he grunted. "Give me my meal or I'll eat you instead."

Josefa swung her stick again, so hard that she knocked off one of Judas's ears. Then she snatched her rosary from her pocket and looped it around his neck.

"Set me free!" he gasped, no longer strong enough to shout the way he had just a second before.

"First, help me to get out of here." Josefa climbed up onto his back. She was just tall enough to scramble out of the hole. When she was safely above ground, she reached down and pulled her rosary up with her.

"Give me back my ear!" Judas shouted.

Josefa laughed. "I'm keeping that for good luck."

The five young women, the hunters, and Josefa set off to see the king. When he saw that his daughters had been rescued from Judas's clutches, he gave them to the hunters to marry. There were just enough princesses to go around—except of course, Josefa was not really a man.

"Your majesty," she told the king, "I cannot marry your daughter."

"What?" the king shouted. "You deserve her more than anyone. Why would a strong and clever man like yourself turn down such an offer?"

"Because I am no man. I am a woman."

"What! You who defeated Judas?"

"Yes."

The king was flabbergasted, and so were the hunters. They could not believe that the one who was braver than all the rest was really a woman. But when Josefa put on woman's clothing again, they finally accepted the truth.

"Next time we have a war," the king said, "I shall make you the captain of all my armies. In the meantime, you shall have whatever share of my riches you desire."

And so Josefa had all that she wanted. She kept Judas's ear locked away, and she had good luck all her life.

his folktale from New Mexico illustrates the Latino belief that despite cultural expectations, women can be just as strong, just as brave, and just as clever as any man—and sometimes, they may be stronger, more courageous, and smarter than all the men around them!

A street mural in Los Angeles portrays the Virgin of Guadalupe.

A Heritage of Contradiction

Latina women have always been strong leaders, passing along their people's traditions, values, and faith. From their Native ancestors, they inherited the belief that women are wise and powerful, offering their unique and valuable contributions to society. At the same time, however, they were expected to follow the Spanish tradition of feminine submission to the strong male. Women's strength was both recognized and honored—and denied.

On the one hand, the symbol for Latino identity is the Virgin of Guadalupe—a woman. She is a powerful cultural image that restored dignity and significance to a downtrodden people. The Virgin takes her place next to La Malinche as a feminine cultural *icon*; where La Malinche has both negative and positive values attached to her, however,

Guadalupe's Story

Christian peasant and Aztec Indian named Juan Diego was walking home on a winter day in 1531 when he saw the Virgin Mary. She was dark skinned, like Juan's people, and she addressed him in Nahuatl, the Aztec language. She said she was "the Mother of the One Great God" and asked to be worshipped by "all the people who live together in this land."

Shortly after this, Juan Diego again encountered the Virgin. She told him to take off his *tilma*, a cape woven from cactus fibers, and fill it with the flowers that were miraculously growing around her feet. He did so—and when he took the flowers to the bishop in Mexico City, everyone could see on his cape an image of the Virgin, just as she had appeared to Juan Diego.

According to tradition, Mary told Juan Diego her name was *Coatlaxopeuh*, which in the Mexica tongue means "one who treads the serpent." To Spaniards hearing the word, it sounded like *Guadalupe*, a famous shrine to the Virgin in Spain. This appearance to Juan Diego became known as Our Lady the Virgin of Guadalupe.

According to believers, Juan Diego's tilma is the one seen today by tens of thousands of pilgrims who visit the Shrine to the Virgin of Guadalupe in Mexico City. The Catholic Church has declared her Patroness (protecting saint) for all the Americas. Almost every household in Mexico, and many more in Central and South America and the United States, has an account of some answer to prayer granted by the Virgin. Her face and form are sometimes seen in the patterns of tortillas, shadows, and tree trunks; when this happens, thousands of people flock to pray before the image.

the Virgin represents the side of womanhood that is both strong *and* pure. She is the mother of all Latinos, and a political symbol that gives courage to the oppressed. Latinos—both men and women—look with reverence and gratitude to this strong feminine figure.

On the other hand, individual Latina women have not often been granted the same respect and honor in their everyday lives. Many have had to keep their strength a secret, hiding it in the long shadows cast by their macho husbands. Native cultures may have valued women's strength, but the European countries that colonized North and South America did not. Though women colonists worked alongside men to build communities in the Western Hemisphere, the male-dominated government and the upper-class society often did not acknowledge their contributions. Instead, women were relegated to the home. They were valued for their homemaking and childrearing skills, but their intelligence was downplayed, and they were considered to be clearly inferior to men.

Latina Women and the Feminist Movement

estern culture downplayed women's contributions for centuries—but in the 1840s, a wave of change washed across North America. The women's movement swelled out of the *abolitionist* movement; feminism was part of a worldview that saw all human beings as equals. Women leaders like Elizabeth Cady Stanton and Lucretia Mott brought about great changes in the United States; their influence was felt in Puerto Rico, Cuba, and other Hispanic nations as well.

Later, however, this first wave of feminist consciousness narrowed its impact, sweeping toward a single goal: suffrage (the right to vote). Once women got the vote, feminism lost its reason for being, and the movement drained away to nothing. American culture continued to define womanhood in terms of *passive* submission to men.

In the 1960s, however, as more and more women took jobs outside the home to help support their families, a second feminist wave crested. Feminists demanded equality for women; they insisted that women were as capable as men; and they sought to raise the consciousness of men and women across North America, while at the same time achieving legal guarantees for women's rights. The movement grew and spread through the sixties and into the seventies.

In the twenty-first century, the feminist movement is no longer as organized, but it has become an insistent force that

Western: *found in or typical of non-Communist countries in Europe, and North and South America, whose culture and government are influenced by Greek and Roman tradition and by Christianity.*

abolitionist: *someone opposed to slavery.*

passive: *not an active participant.*

abhor some of my culture's ways, how it cripples its women, *como burras* [like female donkeys], our strengths used against us, lowly burras bearing humility with dignity. The ability to serve, claim the males, is our highest virtue. I abhor how my culture makes macho caricatures of its men. No, I do not buy all the myths of the tribe into which I was born.
—Gloria Anzaldúa
Borderlands/La Frontera: The New Mestiza

Latina Women and Domestic Abuse

bout one-third of all women experience some form of domestic violence. Most North American agencies attack this problem by seeking to remove the women from danger, while punishing the male offenders. But Latina women look at the situation a little differently. They want to end family violence but not their relationships with their spouses or companions. For them, the family itself has so much value that it deserves to be protected—at all costs. As a result, several agencies have culturally specific programs for Latinos.

For example, in the early 1990s, Julia Perilla started listening to what abused Latina women told her: "Get help for our husbands." An abused wife herself, Perilla was reluctant to change her own approach, but she began to see that these women were right. As a result, she set about finding a way to help the men as well as the women. She has contributed to Alianza, a group of Latino advocates, community activists, practitioners, researchers, and survivors of domestic violence who are working together to find solutions that will end abuse in Latino communities.

Men and women must work together to end domestic abuse, says Adelita Medina, executive director of Alianza. "Why should women carry that responsibility on their own? Domestic violence is a societal problem. Nonviolent men can and should be positive role models for kids and for other men."

Even before the twentieth-century's feminist movement, the Latino community had strong women leaders. Here are a few examples:

- Emma Tenayuca, a famous labor leader in Texas
- María Mercedes Barbudo, jailed in 1824 in Puerto Rico for conspiring against the Spanish
- *las soldaderas*, who fought in the Mexican Revolution of 1910. ("Soldadera" means female soldier.) Soldaderas helped democratize Mexico from a feudal country to one where land was distributed among peasants
- Luisa Capetillo, a Puerto Rican labor organizer and a writer who argued on behalf of equal rights for women
- Dolores Huerta, one of the foremost leaders of the United Farm Workers Union in California

Many Latinas have fought side-by-side in revolutionary struggles in Cuba, Nicaragua, and El Salvador, and they have worked to unionize miners and farmworkers in the Southwest, as well as garment workers in the Northeast. A modern example of a strong woman leader is Antonia

Pantoja, founder of the Puerto Rican Association for Community Affairs, who emphasizes collective decision making, the development of new leaders (especially among the youth), and the good of the group over the personal gain of the individual. Another example is Esperanza Martell, co-founder of the Latin Women's Collective in New York City, a political activist organization that works on behalf of women's issues.

will not be quelled. Although women have still not achieved total equality with men, women have changed the way they think about themselves and their expectations of life. Gender roles are no longer as clearly defined, and men have also altered their thinking about themselves and their relationships with women.

The movement has become a tidal wave, surging around the world. The Latino community, both within the United States and in its native lands, has been influenced as well. Tradition is strong for Latinos, and the family is all-important—but Latinas (women who claim their identity as both women and Latinos) are finding ways to be true to themselves both as women and as Hispanic Americans. In *Borderlands/La Frontera: The New Mestiza*, Gloria Anzaldúa writes of her own experience as a feminist Latina:

I want the freedom to carve and chisel my own face. . . . And if going home [returning to the traditions of her childhood] is denied me then I will have to stand and claim my space, making a new culture—*una cultura mestiza*—with my own lumber, my own bricks and mortar and my own feminist architecture.

entrepreneurs: people who assume the risks and costs of running a business.

posole: a thick Mexican soup made with hominy, chicken or pork, chilies, and cilantro.

Today, many Hispanic American families depend on the income of both partners in order to make ends meet. As a result, women leave their homes for many different kinds of jobs—and they experience more freedom and financial independence. As Dr. Ana Nogales says, "Many Latinas are discovering that in addition to being competent mothers and housewives, they can also be competent workers, great supervisors, successful *entrepreneurs*. . . . They want success in a career and economic independence." Having to care for their families while holding down a job brings stresses, just as it does for all women across America, but it also brings a sense of dignity and worth. Latina women can no longer be dismissed as quiet and submissive domestic laborers.

Modern Latinas

In today's world—whether it be the financial world, the entertainment world, or the art world—Latinas are no longer on the fringes of power; instead, they are a burning and creative force whose power is growing. Like Josefa, the heroine in the New Mexican folktale that began this chapter, they demonstrate their intelligence and courage in countless ways.

In the music world, for example, Gloria Estefan has become a household name; she went from being a Cuban refugee to having a $170 million fortune. Her concerts are contemporary, professional, and slick—and yet they demonstrate traditional Hispanic family values with big-screen photo albums of Gloria's baby pictures, her parents, her husband, and her children.

A typical roadside restaurant in Chimayo, New Mexico

In the literary world, Latina authors like Isabel Allende, Sandra Cisneros, and Gloria Anzaldúa write bestsellers that allow readers to enter the magical and colorful worlds the authors inhabit. Their works give voice to the real-life concerns of their Latina sisters, and as a result, Americans have become more conscious of feminist issues, while glimpsing the beauty and mystery of Latino traditions.

Most Latina women will never be famous, of course. And yet many of them are quietly and surely building something that enriches the world. Leona Medina-Tiede, owner of a restaurant in Chimayo, New Mexico, is a good example.

The eldest daughter of a family of eleven, Leona grew up helping her uncle run a fruit stand in the summer; during the week before Easter, she helped her mother sell homemade tortillas and bowls of *posole* to pilgrims who came to the religious shrine in Chimayo. As an adult, Leona opened her own roadside stand on New Mexico's Highway

Leona with her grandchildren in her restaurant

76, where she sold homemade Mexican food. Seven years later, she began mass-producing her tortillas. Her day began at four in the morning; she took a break to go to Mass, and then worked for the rest of the day in her little restaurant.

Eventually, she and her husband converted a storage shed near the Sanctuary of Chimayo into a take-out restaurant. She staffed her new business with family members and worked hard to make it a success. Thirty-seven years later, her business is still thriving; if you go there and ask for your favorite Mexican food, chances are one of Leona's children or grandchildren will take your order. All year round, twenty hours a day, seven days a week, her tortilla machine produces about forty thousand tortillas a day. Slow cookers filled with beans simmer on the countertops—and Leona's warm smile welcomes visitors and makes them feel at home. The voices of her family fill the small restaurant, and even her youngest grandchildren obviously take pride in their grandmother's achievement. They may inherit their share in the successful business Leona has created—but they will also inherit something far more important: a legacy of strength, determination, and love.

Leona had the stamina and courage to pursue a dream. In the process, however, she never turned her back on the traditional values that fueled her resolve—faith and family. For Leona, as for many Latina women, faith is interwoven through all of life—and family is the very center of that life.

Everyone should be a feminist. If the world was perfect, we wouldn't even have a name for feminism. People wouldn't be sexist and they wouldn't discriminate, but that's just not how it is. There's still more to be done.
—Sabina Mora, Argentine feminist

Habla Español

cultura (cool-too-rah): culture

mujer (moo-hair): woman

5

The Family

The concept of family is the structure
that shapes much of Hispanic life. Both
men and women—whether traditionally
macho and submissive, or modern and liber-
ated—set family as one of the highest priorities in
their lives. Children grow up with an appreciation and
respect for their parents, their grandparents, and their
aunts and uncles; brothers and sisters, as well as cousins and
other relatives, do what they can to help and support each other.
As long as a person has a family, he will never be without resources.

This sense of family is played out in countless ways, both big and
small. From the smallest acts of everyday life, to the once-in-a-lifetime traditions families celebrate together, family gives meaning to Latino life. The
quinceañera is just one example of this.

The Quinceañera

t's perfect," says Addilene Hinojoza as she looks in a mirror at a fancy dress, one that took her six months to find. "It's the prettiest thing I've ever seen." Addilene is preparing for her quinceañera, the Latino celebration that marks a girl's passage into womanhood on her fifteenth birthday. (Scheri Smith writes about Addilene's quinceañera in an article in the Louisville, Kentucky *Courier-Journal*.)

According to long-held traditions, quinceañeras contain three main components: a Mass (or religious service), a party, and a dance with family members. The roots of this celebration come from both Spanish court dances and Aztec coming-of-age ceremonies.

Addie's parents, Petronilo and Concepcion Hinojoza, have ten children; Addie is the youngest, and the first in the family to have a quinceañera, since these events often cost as much as a wedding. Such an expense would have been too much for the Hinojozas to afford until now.

Thirteen years ago, the Hinojoza family left Mexico, moving first to California and then to Kentucky. Addie doesn't remember Mexico but she dreams of it. "Mexico is the most wonderful place in the world," she says. "My parents left for us and I'll try to pay them back by trying to be a good person."

Addie's older siblings had to drop out of school to go to work. She will be the first to finish high school, as well as the first to celebrate her coming of age in the traditional way. The family is proud of their youngest child.

All the plans and arrangements for Addie's quinceañera took a full year, and it is truly a family event. Relatives around the country contributed whatever money they could afford to make the celebration possible. Family members came to Kentucky to attend the party from as far away as California.

The quinceañera is the special sort of day that only happens once in a girl's life; eventually, life will have to go back to normal for Addie. She will no longer be the center of attention—but Addilene Hinojoza will never be alone. As long as she lives, she will have her own place in the large and close-knit family that loves her.

Multigenerational Families

ociologists consider the typical U.S. family to be a *nuclear* family. Parents are the nucleus and the children gravitate like electrons around them. Nowadays, some U.S. families are even smaller, with a single parent instead of two. But Latino families tend to be much larger—what sociologists call the *extended* family.

Most Hispanic American families are made up of several generations of family members and their siblings. They may live near one another, or actually share a house. In any case, they maintain close ties. Dr. Ana Nogales writes: "Without the cousins, *abuelas*, sisters and *tíos* whom we can automatically trust with our personal problems, we feel isolated and alone."

The Latino family includes grandparents. Traditionally, *los abuelos* helped around the home by doing chores such as cooking or housekeeping. In the United States, where many Hispanic mothers work outside the home, grandparents often provide a valuable service: in more than one out of ten Latino households, young children are cared for by their grandparents during the day while their parents work.

Parientes are also an important part of la familia. These are blood relatives like *tías* and tíos (aunts and uncles) and *primos* (cousins). No matter how distant the connection, relatives are part of the family unit. For example, if you are Latino, the children of your grandmother's cousin might be introduced as family.

Some family members are not related by blood. Godparents—or *padrinos*—are respected friends of the parents, chosen to help rear the children. Godparents are expected to assist in the child's spiritual development, and if the parents should die while the children are young, the padrinos will raise them. A godchild—or *ahijada*—will treat her padrinos with love, honor, and respect.

Hispanic families value their children.

Families in all cultures cherish children, but Latinos do so especially. The fertility rate for women born in Mexico is more than twice that of Anglo women. While Anglo and Asian families usually assume it is the parents' responsibility to raise children, Latinos expect everyone—grandparents, aunts, uncles, godparents—to instruct, correct, and care for children. Home is often a warm and nurturing place, and in many Latino households, grown children stay home until they are married.

Children treat the elders in their families with respect and honor. This means they obey their parents, grandparents, and aunts and uncles. If told something, they listen carefully, with eyes downcast to show submission. Arguing back is rude. In return, children know they can approach their elders with *confianza* (trust). Confianza means a

Older Latinos offer support to the younger generation.

Latino young person always has family members to whom he can go with problems—whether for advice, financial help, or simply emotional support.

An everyday incident in a Latino neighborhood illustrates the ways Hispanic families work. Several children were walking to school when a man on his front porch made vulgar gestures to them. That evening, a group of men—the father, uncles, and cousins of the children—walked together down the street and confronted the man. The rude incident was never repeated. An Anglo family might have been more inclined to call the police, but in this Latino neighborhood, members of *la familia* handled such matters.

The Negative Consequences of Many Children

pension: retirement pay.

The Latino trend toward large families has a darker side as well. When women have children close together, they are in the position of caring for two or more infants or toddlers at the same time—a highly demanding task that leaves women with little time or energy for anything else. Furthermore, when women have numerous pregnancies in a short period, they are less able to physically, emotionally, and financially recuperate between children. This can put stress on the entire family.

To make matters more difficult, economic circumstances require that most Hispanic women work outside the home. This creates a double burden for them, because their responsibilities within the house do not decrease when they get jobs outside the home; few Latino men are willing to contribute to household responsibilities. Although most Hispanic women will have the support of their extended families, many of these family members may be in the same situation, juggling the demands of family and career. The situation is even harder for single-parent families.

As with other American families, women are the heads of some Hispanic households. Unfortunately, these households are more likely to face poverty than are two-parent or male-headed households. When husbands die or leave, women may be left with many children, no work experience, and few resources. Women who have only worked at home do not have their own *pension* plans, so if their husband dies, they may be left without

According to a Centers for Disease Control and Prevention's 2002 study, Hispanic women in the United States have a total fertility rate (the average number of children a woman will have in her lifetime) of 3.1, well above the national average of 2.1 births per woman.

According to the American Association of University Women, some Latino women who want an education and a career are sometimes chastised by their own families for turning their backs on their families, forgetting their roots, or trying to be Anglo.

financial support. Even if they can find work, single-parent households only have one adult wage earner—and women make less money than men. Factors like these contribute to higher poverty levels in female-headed households, and poverty remains a formidable problem for many Hispanic families.

A Source of Strength

Although the Latino family has many positive qualities, like any family, it is not perfect. People who live closely together inevitably hurt each other in a variety ways. Overall, however, their sense of family is a source of identity and strength for many Hispanic Americans.

Like Addie Hinojoza's family, Latino families are bound more tightly by the special occasions they celebrate together. At the heart of these celebrations—including the quinceañera—lies a deep faith in the supernatural world. Reality is a place of mystery and amazement; this conviction gives warmth and light to many Hispanic families, and it serves to strengthen and affirm their bonds with each other.

𝖧abla 𝖤spañol

familia (fah-meel-ee-ah): family

abuelos (ah-bway-lows): grandparents

tías/tíos (tee-ahs/tee-ohs): aunts/uncles

primos (pree-moes): cousins

padrinos (pah-dree-noes): godparents

BARBARA CORNELIO ZALDIVAR

DESCAN
SA EN
EN
P
A
Z

A World Full
of Wonder

Rafa Fuentes watched the flicker of candle-
light over his family's faces. Everyone he loved
was here, right where he could see them: his mother
and father, his two little sisters, and his grandfather.
Other people were here too, people Rafa couldn't see—his
grandma who died last winter, his brother who died when
Rafa was still a baby, and his other grandparents who had gone to
heaven when Rafa's mother was a teenager.

A Day of the Dead altar

And there were other guests present as well, people so familiar they seemed like part of the Fuentes family: César Chávez, the civil rights leader who died the same year Rafa was born, and Selena, the beautiful singer who was murdered when Rafa was just a little kid. The small room was alive with souls; Rafa thought he could almost see them in the dance of light and shadow cast by the many candles that lit each *ofrenda*.

The ofrendas were altars, little tables Rafa and his sisters had helped decorate, the way they did each year. Cut-paper designs hung in bright festoons from the ceiling over each candle-lit altar, and the family had carefully arranged the dead's favorite things amid the candles. Some of the objects were old familiar friends they saw every year: their brother's favorite toy, their grandparents' books, Grandma's knitting needles, the photos of each person. Other things he and his family had made special this year: drawings for their brother, notes to their grandma, the special dishes Mamá made each year for her parents so they could enjoy the taste and scent of their favorite foods. Mamá had also made *pan de muerto*—the sweet bread for the dead—and bought sugar skulls for the children. Rafa and his sisters placed bouquets of marigolds on every altar and hung paper skeletons from all the doorways.

Rafa looked up at his favorite skeleton, the one that hung directly opposite his place on the sofa. The skeleton seemed to wink and grin back at him, and Rafa had to smile. He remembered how sad he had been when his grandma had died, but now he no longer felt so bad. Grandma was right here in the room with them, the way she had always been every other year—but this year, she was one of the beloved dead. The skeleton's grin was comforting, somehow, as though death were a delightful joke; for a moment, Rafa thought he heard his grandma's laughter.

An Ancient Tradition

Long ago, the Natives of *Mesoamerica* believed that once a year the souls of the deceased were allowed to return from the world of the dead. During that special time, they could keep company with their loved ones and enjoy again the ordinary pleasures found in the world of the living. The Natives were convinced that the two worlds were equally real and

Mesoamerica: a region of Central America and southern North America that was occupied by several civilizations, predominantly the Maya, during the pre-Columbia era.

Cut-paper skulls celebrate the Day of the Dead.

sacrilegious: relating to the treatment of a holy object with disrespect.

pagan: heathen; having to do with a religion that worships more than one god.

equally important; they were merely separated by a door, a door that swung open once a year.

To guide the dead souls, their loved ones lit fires. They also strewed the way with marigold blossoms, blooms that would catch the eye with their brightness and tickle the nose with their pungent scent, reminding the dead of the earth where they once lived. People placed bowls of water for thirsty souls, parched after their journey from the other world, and they spread out the dead's favorite foods for their enjoyment. The month-long celebration was a time of laughter and feasting. Skulls smiled down on festivities from their places of honor; for these long-ago people, the skull was a symbol of hope, like an arrow pointing toward resurrection and new life in eternity.

When the Spanish arrived in the land that would be modern-day Mexico, the people there had been celebrating this ancient tradition for more than three thousand years. The Spanish took death very seriously, however, and they were shocked by this lighthearted attitude to something they perceived as a grim and terrifying reality. They considered the celebration to be *sacrilegious* and *pagan*. As they set about converting the Natives to Christianity, the Spanish tried to destroy the celebration.

But the Native people would not let go of either their belief or their practice. Finally, the Spanish allowed them to continue their celebrations, but the Catholic priests moved the tradition from the summer to November 2, All Soul's Day, the day set aside by the Church for remembering the dead. *Día de Los Muertos* then evolved into a holiday practiced throughout Mexico and the Southwest. Today many people in Latin America and the United States honor this tradition, and the practice is growing among Hispanic American communities of all nationalities.

Pan de Muerto

Common Threads

Some people claim that Day of the Dead celebrations represent a clash between Christianity and ancient pagan religions—but others see the holiday as an affirmation of a common faith shared by both perspectives. Although European culture has traditionally faced death with sorrow and dread, Christianity itself claims that death cannot destroy love . . . and that death is the threshold to eternal life. The laughter and partying at a Day of the Dead celebration is more true to this faith than sadness and fear would be.

Magic and Mystery
Around Every Corner

he faith and attitudes Latinos celebrate on the Day of the Dead are not once-a-year beliefs; instead, many Hispanic Americans live their entire lives with an awareness of the supernatural world. Even the most ordinary of days may be touched with wonder: while scrubbing the kitchen floor, a woman reads in the soapsuds a message from her departed husband; a man is driving home from the office, preoccupied with work worries, when the truck in front of him explodes—but Saint Barbara pushes on his foot, helping him brake in time to avoid the fire; a child who dashes in front of a car is pulled to safety by the strong but shadowy hands of a watchful angel. Most Latinos believe that occurrences like these are very real and very common. Magical and miraculous things can happen at any moment.

Because they believe the supernatural world is so close to the one where we live, Latinos often perceive meaning and patterns in ordinary objects. Jesus may show his face in a cloud; Mary may appear in the speckles and creases on a tortilla; coins and feathers and sudden breezes may all be love tokens from those who have crossed into the next world. As a result, Latino religion is not the dry, weekly practice that many Anglos experience. Hispanic Americans live their faith moment by moment, with a sharp awareness of all that is strange and wonderful.

Miraculous moments may involve events that are intimate and personal—or they may be experienced by the entire community. For example, certain churches in the Southwest have long traditions of miracles.

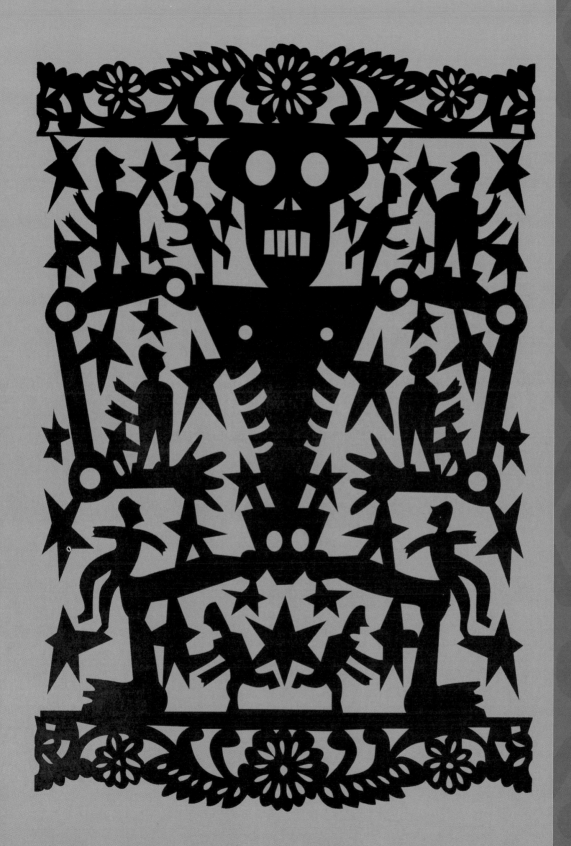

Each straw cross woven into the fence represents a prayer.

El Santuario de Chimayó

early two hundred years ago, in the small village of Chimayó in New Mexico, a monk was praying when he saw light bursting from a hillside. Amazed and excited, he began to dig into the hill. Buried in the earth was a crucifix.

A local priest brought the crucifix to Santa Cruz, but three times it disappeared and was later found back in its hole. By the third time, everyone understood that it wanted to remain in Chimayó, and so a small chapel was built on the site. People came from far and near to see the mysterious image of Christ—and those who were sick were healed, while those who were sad found joy. The miracles grew so numerous that more and more people came to the tiny chapel.

Hispanic Americans believe the church is built on sacred earth; the soil there is thought to possess miraculous healing powers. The crucifix that began it all still resides on the chapel altar, but it is the "sacred sand pit" from which it sprang that draws *pilgrims*. Each year during Holy Week (the week before Easter), thousands of people journey to Chimayó to visit the Santuario and take away a little of the holy dirt. They weave straw crosses through the chain-link fence that surrounds the sanctuary, and each cross represents a prayer. Many claim their prayers are answered.

pilgrims: people who travel to worship at a shrine.

El Santuario de Chimayo

A Painting with a Magical Glow

In the tiny town of Rancho de Taos stands another, still more ancient church, the Church of San Francisco de Asis. It holds several treasures, holy objects from the seventeenth and eighteenth centuries, but what draws believers most powerfully is a more recent painting.

The Shadow of the Cross, painted in 1896 by a French-Canadian artist named Henri Ault, shows the life-size figure of Christ standing by the Sea of Galilee. When the painting is in

95

A shrine to the Virgin of Guadalupe is surrounded by the symbols of individuals' faith.

The church of San Francisco de Asis

the light, Jesus is surrounded by wispy white clouds in a pale blue sky. It's a rather ordinary religious painting.

But in the darkness, the painting reveals something altogether different. The figure of Jesus appears three dimensional, and the form of the cross appears over his left shoulder. What is most amazing, though, is the light that glows from the sky, from the halo that surrounds Christ's head, and from the sea, as though an unseen moon were shedding its light over the entire scene. No one has been able to explain the strange luminescence that has lasted for more than a hundred years.

A Sense of Wonder

Some might say that Latinos are a superstitious people, seeing and believing things that really aren't there. Such a statement would be a value judgment based on a cultural bias that may be just as restricting as any superstition.

Many of the most vital Hispanic traditions are built on an assumption that life is full of amazing possibilities: dead family members may join their loved ones in the living room; the saints commune regularly with those on earth; and God reveals himself in tangible and daily ways. This attitude toward life is very different from that of the Western world, where much thought is based on the scientific method.

All human beings, however, struggle to understand how life works. They look for patterns that will help them predict how they should live their lives in relation to the ongoing flow of events. These beliefs eventually give individuals—and cultures—a mental roadway to follow through life. They help people feel comfortable in the midst of life's chaos.

Many Americans rely on science for their roadway. According to current thought, science proves what is real and disproves what is false; it has the ultimate say on how we see and shape reality. In a world ruled by the scientific method, there seems to be little room for magic and miracles.

But other cultures—including the Latino culture—have ancient traditions that look at the world quite differently. They approach life from a different perspective, with a different set of expectations; they use a different roadway to maneuver through life.

This roadway looks to the supernatural world for signposts. Other individuals may dismiss these as foolish or superstitious—but these miraculous markers of another world

he further you go in school, the more you hear about the scientific method, a premise that is basic to our society's understanding of how the world works. A person using the scientific method will follow these steps:

1. She will formulate a problem.
2. She will collect data through observation and experiments. (This data must be based on things that can be observed with the senses and measured.)
3. She will create a hypothesis, a sort of educated guess or assumption that will explain the results she obtained through observation and experiment.
4. She will test and confirm her hypothesis, again using results that can be observed with the senses and measured. If her hypothesis proves to be false, she will formulate a new hypothesis and proceed from there.

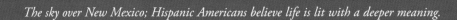

The sky over New Mexico; Hispanic Americans believe life is lit with a deeper meaning.

provide Latinos with a powerful sense of life's meaning. Faith in a world of wonder unites them as families and as a vital cultural group. It gives them hope to face the challenges of their lives.

Victor Villaseñor, author of *Walking Stars*, expresses this concept with these words:

If you have the eyes to see and the ears to hear, you will know that to live your life without the magic of your God-given soul is to live life like a fish out of water, like an eagle without a sky. . . . You see, the soul is to magic just like the eagle is to the sky, and the fish is to water . . . our soul is fearless and full of joy and makes living a great, glorious, magical adventure open to all!

. . . We're all angels . . . full-time spiritual beings feeling a little human while we live in this short, tiny dream called life, la vida.

Miracles of Love

Author Victor Villaseñor describes the conflict he experienced between living in the modern, scientific world and the traditional world of his Latino heritage:

No matter how open I was now to what my parents told me, I still got stumped by their reality, especially when they used words like "miracles," "angels," "God," . . . so often that it just seemed ridiculous to my modern-thinking mind. Why, they spoke of each new day as though it were a magical gift from God, a daily miracle of love, offered to us on the wings of angels by the Almighty. And the sun was the Right Eye of God. Boy, it just seemed too flowery and romantic to me, and it really had nothing to do with basic reality, as they kept insisting.

. . . And, suddenly, I glanced around and the whole world looked so different, so beautiful and full of magic. I looked up at the sky and felt better than I'd felt in years. It was as if I'd finally come home within myself for the first time in a long, long time.

Latinos love to celebrate (maybe because they see the world as giving them so many miracles to enjoy), and their years are full of special days. Here is a list:

RELIGIOUS HOLIDAYS:
6 de enero/January 6: El Dia de los Reyes Magos
(Day of the Magi Kings)

Throughout Latin America, this is the day children get their gifts, rather than on Christmas Day itself. That makes sense, since this day commemorates the wise men who came bearing gifts for the newborn Christ Child.

Abril/April: Semana Santa (Holy Week)

This is the week before Easter. In many U.S. cities, one can see processions where statues or actors portray the events of Christ's Passion.

Agosto/August 1 to 6: The Feast of Salvador del Mundo
(The Feast of the Savior of the World)

Salvadorans in California, Florida, and New Jersey have special Masses and processions honoring Christ on this day.

*8 de septiembre/September 8: Día de La Caridad del Cobre
(Day of the Virgin of Charity of Copper)*

Cubans celebrate the day that a miraculous statue of the Virgin appeared to three men from a copper mine.

*18 de octubre/October 18: Señor de Los Milagros
(Lord of Miracles)*

Peruvians celebrate the discovery of a statue of Christ, which amazingly survived an earthquake.

*2 de noviembre/November 2: Dia de Los Muertos
(Day of the Dead; see pages 87–90)*

*12 de diciembre/December 12: Día de la Virgen
de Guadalupe (Day of the Virgin of Guadalupe)*

Special Masses and processions celebrate the appearance of the Virgin to Juan Diego.

diciembre/December 16 to 24: Las Posadas (The Inns)

A Mexican custom recalling the Holy Family's futile search for an inn. Families go door to door, asking for lodging. They are turned away, but given treats as they leave.

24 de deciembre/December 24: Noche Buena (Good Night)
Gatherings the night before Christmas focus on family and
the birth of the Christ Child.

25 de deciembre/December 25: Navidad (Nativity)
Christmas Day is not as big in Latin America as it is in the
United States, since gifts are given on the Day of the Three
Kings. Many Latinos in the United States have adapted to
the North American custom.

SECULAR HOLIDAYS

*10 de enero/January 10: aniversario del cumpleaños de
(Anniversary of the birthday of) Eugenio Maria de Hostos*
Puerto Ricans celebrate the birth of this patriot and educa-
tor. New York City Schools schedule a vacation day on this
date to focus on Puerto Rican heritage.

28 de enero/January 28:
aniversario del cumpleaños de José Martí
The birthday of José Martí, Cuban poet and patriot.
Miami schools close in his honor.

*27 de febrero /Febuary 27: Dia del Independencia
(Dominican Republic Independence Day).*

21 de marzo /March 21:
aniversario del cumpleaños de Benito Júarez

May 5: Cinco de Mayo
The fifth of May when Mexican Americans celebrate the victory of the Mexican army against French forces at the Battle of Puebla in 1862. You should see the all-out festivities around Olvera Street in Los Angeles!

20 de Mayo/May 20: Dia del Independencia
(Cuban Independence Day)

Second Sunday in June:
National Puerto Rican Parade Day
Over 3 million spectators line up for the parade along Manhattan's Fifth Avenue.

12 de octubre / October 12: El Dia de la Raza
(Day of the People)
Celebrates the day when Columbus arrived in the New World, an event that led to the creation of Latino identity.

Timeline

1400s—The Spanish become the first Europeans to come to the Americas.

October 12, 1492—The first Europeans encounter the Native Indian world of the Americas, thus giving birth to the Hispanic culture.

1517—Cortés arrives on the Yucatan Peninsula.

1531—Our Lady the Virgin of Guadalupe appears to Juan Diego.

1824—María Mercedes Barbudo is jailed in Puerto Rico for conspiring against the Spanish.

1840s—Feminism sweeps across North America.

1896—*The Shadow of the Cross* painted by Henri Ault.

1960s—A second wave of feminism covers North America.

1980s—The U.S. government introduces the term "Hispanic."

January 2003—The U.S. Census Bureau announces that Hispanics have become the country's largest minority group.

Further Reading

Anzaldúa, Gloria. *Borderlands/La Frontera: The New Mestiza*. San Francisco: Aunt Lute Books, 1999.

Ballesteros, Octavio A. and María del Carmen Ballesteros. *Mexican Sayings: The Treasure of a People*. Austin, Tex.: Eakin Press, 1992.

Bierhorst, John. *Latin American Folktales: Stories from Hispanic and Indian Traditions*. New York: Pantheon, 2000.

Manard, Valerie. *The Latino Holiday Book*. New York: Marlowe and Company, 2000.

Villaseñor, Victor. *Walking Stars: Stories of Magic and Power*. New York: Doubleday, 1994.

For More Information

Day of the Dead
www.azcentral.com/ent/dead

Day of the Dead in Mexico
www.dayofthedead.com

Hispanic Culture
www.hispanic-research.com/home/hispanic_culture.htm

Hispanic Heritage Plaza
www.hispaniconline.com

La Llorona
www.lallorona.com

The Weeping Woman
www.legendsofamerica.com/HC-WeepingWoman1.html

Publisher's note:
The Web sites listed on this page were active at the time of publication. The publisher is not responsible for Web sites that have changed their addresses or discontinued operation since the date of publication. The publisher will review and update the Web site list upon each reprint.

Index

Picture Credits

Benjamin Stewart: pp. 37, 46, 49, 56, 60, 73, 74, 94, 95, 97, 99, 100

Corel: p. 20

Dianne Hodack: p. 6

Imageexpress.com: pp. 13, 23, 30 (top and bottom), 53, 55, 66, 69, 78, 82

Marsha McIntosh: pp. 81, 85

Micaela Sanna: p. 89

Michelle Bouch: pp. 24, 26, 29, 31, 32, 33, 39, 50, 93

PhotoDisc: pp. 40, 45

Photos.com: pp. 15, 34, 59, 77, 87

Santuario de Chimayó, photographer Benjamin Stewart: pp. 8, 22, 44, 58, 76, 86

Sarah Elizabeth Garland: pp. 88, 91

Museum of Spanish Colonial Art, Santa Fe, N.M., photographer Benjamin Stewart: pp. 9, 10, 16,

Biographies

Ellyn Sanna is the author of many nonfiction and fiction books, for both children and adults, including several books in the Mason Crest series NORTH AMERICAN FOLK-LORE. She has traveled in both Mexico and South America, and spent most of a year living and working in an orphanage in Tijuana, Mexico. She has always loved the Spanish language and the people who speak it.

Dr. José E. Limón is professor of Mexican-American Studies at the University of Texas at Austin where he has taught for twenty-five years. He has authored over forty articles and three books on Latino cultural studies and history. He lectures widely to academic audiences, civic groups, and K–12 educators.